NBA's TOP 10 DUOS

BY WILL GRAVES

NBA's TOP 10

SportsZone

An Imprint of Abdo Publishing
abdopublishing.com

abdopublishing.com

Published by Abdo Publishing, a division of ABDO, PO Box 398166, Minneapolis, Minnesota 55439.

Printed in the United States of America, North Mankato, Minnesota
042018
092018

THIS BOOK CONTAINS RECYCLED MATERIALS

Cover Photo: John W. McDonough/Sports Illustrated/Getty Images
Interior Photos: Rich Pedroncelli/AP Images, 4–5; Marcio Jose Sanchez/Zuma Press/Icon Sportswire, 7; AP Images, 8, 16; Kevin Reece/Icon Sportswire, 9; Marvin E. Newman/Sports Illustrated/Getty Images, 11; Eric Gay/AP Images, 13, 20; Steve Lipofsky/Sports Illustrated/Getty Images, 15; Herb Scharfman/Sports Illustrated/Getty Images, 17; Andy Hayt/Sports Illustrated/Getty Images, 19; Mark J. Terrill/AP Images, 21; Roberto Borea/AP Images, 23; Michael Conroy/AP Images, 25; Ray Stubblebine/Reuters/Newscom, 26; Beth A. Keiser/AP Images, 27

Editor: Bradley Cole
Series Designer: Craig Hinton

Library of Congress Control Number: 2017962571

Publisher's Cataloging-in-Publication Data

Names: Graves, Will, author.
Title: NBA's top 10 duos / by Will Graves.
Other titles: NBA's top ten duos
Description: Minneapolis, Minnesota : Abdo Publishing, 2019. | Series: NBA's top 10 |Includes online resources and index.
Identifiers: ISBN 9781532114502 (lib.bdg.) | ISBN 9781532154331 (ebook)
Subjects: LCSH: Sports teams--Juvenile literature. | Basketball--Records--United States--Juvenile literature. | Basketball--History--Juvenile literature. | National Basketball Association--Juvenile literature.
Classification: DDC 796.323--dc23

TABLE OF CONTENTS

INTRODUCTION

There are five players on the court for each team during a National Basketball Association (NBA) game. Sometimes, it just takes two players to take over a game. The league's history is filled with great teams built around two players who worked well together.

Sometimes dynamic duos played the same position. Walt Frazier and Earl Monroe were two guards who sped the New York Knicks to a pair of championships. Guards Stephen Curry and Klay Thompson nailed shots from all over the floor for the Golden State Warriors.

Sometimes, these duos couldn't be more different. In Utah, efficient point guard John Stockton and muscular forward Karl Malone powered the Utah Jazz. They found a way to make it work on the floor. They made each other and their teammates better. Along the way, they celebrated as champions and changed the NBA forever. Make way for some of the greatest duos in basketball history.

10

STEPHEN CURRY & KLAY THOMPSON

Steph Curry and Klay Thompson arrived in the NBA eager to prove they could play the game just as well as their dads.

Dell Curry poured in 1,245 three-pointers during his 16-year career. Mychal Thompson won a pair of championship rings while playing center for the Los Angeles Lakers in the 1980s.

It turns out their sons could play a little ball, too. Thompson joined Curry on the Golden State Warriors in 2012. It did not take long for the two guards to drive defenses crazy with their long-range shooting. They earned the nickname "The Splash Brothers" for the way they could send the ball splashing through the net after another three-point shot.

With Curry and Thompson taking shots from all over, the Warriors made the playoffs for just the second time in 19 seasons in 2013. Curry led the NBA in three-pointers that season. Thompson was third. The two were just getting started.

Curry and Thompson would often try to one-up each other. In 2015, Curry won the three-point contest during All-Star Weekend. The next year, Thompson took home top honors.

SPLASH BROTHERS

Steph Curry and Klay Thompson have wasted little time rewriting the NBA record book. Heading into the 2017–18 season, Curry held the top three spots for the most three-pointers made in the regular season. He made an incredible 402 during the 2015–16 season, the most ever. Number 4 on the list? Thompson, who made 276 during that same year.

Klay Thompson, *left*, and Stephen Curry celebrate an NBA Championship in 2016.

In 2015, Curry and Thompson led Golden State to the franchise's first NBA title since 1975. The following season, the Warriors set an NBA record by winning 73 games. Superstar forward Kevin Durant became an honorary third Splash Brother when he signed with the Warriors in 2016. The "brotherhood" was now a threesome, and Golden State cut down the net a third time as champions.

09

Point guard Walt Frazier, *right,* was known for his scoring and his incredible defense.

WALT FRAZIER & EARL MONROE

Walt Frazier and Earl Monroe were stars long before they became teammates. The two guards played the game with flash and style.

Frazier joined the New York Knicks in 1967. A Knicks trainer gave him the nickname "Clyde," while a sportswriter called Monroe "Earl the Pearl" during his college days. The nickname followed Monroe to the NBA's Baltimore Bullets, who selected Monroe with the second pick in 1967. The Knicks took Frazier three spots later.

They spent four years battling each other as opponents before the Knicks traded for Monroe during the 1971–72 season.

It took time for the former rivals to figure out how to play together. The Knicks lost to the Los Angeles Lakers in the 1972 NBA Finals. While Frazier averaged 23.0 points per game in the Finals, Monroe averaged just 6.8 points while dealing with a heel injury.

Earl Monroe drives to the basket.

The following year, Monroe was healthy, and things started to click for the Knicks. Frazier and Monroe started to understand that if they shared the spotlight with each other, New York could be unstoppable.

Together, they dominated the NBA. Frazier led the defense. Monroe rediscovered the slashing style that made him an All-Star while playing for the Bullets. They became known as the "Rolls Royce Backcourt" because they played with class and style that no other guards in the league could match.

A rematch with the Lakers awaited in the 1973 Finals. This time, Monroe was healthy, and the Knicks were ready. Monroe scored a team-high 23 points in a Game 5 victory that gave New York the title. The former rivals were now champions together.

08

Jerry West passes the ball to Elgin Baylor.

JERRY WEST & ELGIN BAYLOR

Jerry West and Elgin Baylor grew up not too far from each other on the East Coast. Baylor was from Washington, DC. West called the hills of West Virginia home. They became teammates almost 3,000 miles (4,800 km) away under the bright lights of Los Angeles.

Baylor was a budding star known for his high-flying moves. West joined Baylor when the Minneapolis Lakers selected the sharp-shooting guard with the second pick in the 1960 draft before relocating to Los Angeles.

Baylor was called "Mr. Inside." He changed the way the game is played with his vast array of moves. He could score with ease from all over the court.

West was called "Mr. Outside" while becoming one of the best shooters in NBA history. Fans also called him "Mr. Clutch." West always seemed to come through when the game was on the line. When the NBA created a new logo to represent the league in 1969, it modeled the logo after a picture of West dribbling the ball. It is still the logo today.

The only thing West and Baylor didn't do together was win a title. They had plenty of chances. The Lakers reached seven NBA Finals with West

ON AND OFF THE COURT

Jerry West and Elgin Baylor weren't just close on the court, but also on the stat sheet. Baylor averaged 27.4 points during his career. West averaged 27.0. West played in 14 All-Star Games, with Baylor making it 11 times. They reached the Hall of Fame three years apart and were both named to the 50 Greatest Players in NBA History list in 1996.

and Baylor on the roster. They lost all seven times, with six of the defeats coming to the rival Boston Celtics.

07

Tim Duncan, *left*, holds up his Finals MVP trophy and David Robinson holds up the championship trophy.

DAVID ROBINSON & TIM DUNCAN

In the summer of 1997, some San Antonio Spurs fans worried if their town was big enough for both David Robinson and Tim Duncan. They couldn't have been more wrong.

Robinson was the face of the franchise in the 1990s. The 7-foot-1 center was called the Admiral because he graduated from the US Naval Academy and served two years in the Navy before joining the Spurs. Robinson made up for lost time. In 1990 he was the NBA Rookie of the Year at 25 years old. He quickly became a fixture on the All-Star team.

A bad break for Robinson during the 1996–97 season led to a good break for the Spurs. With "The Admiral" sidelined for much of the season due to multiple injuries, the Spurs finished with the third-worst record in the league. As a result they ended up with the top pick in the 1997 Draft.

Duncan, a 6-foot-11 forward who starred at Wake Forest, was the best player available. Like Robinson, he was quick for his size. Like Robinson, Duncan didn't crave attention. Like Robinson, Duncan made sure to put the team's needs above his own.

Head coach Gregg Popovich was convinced that Duncan and Robinson could work together. He couldn't have been more right. The "Twin Towers"

wasted little time taking on the rest of the NBA. Duncan won Rookie of the Year in 1997–98, eight years after Robinson won the same award.

The following season, Robinson and Duncan powered the Spurs to their first NBA title. They won it all again in 2003, the final season of Robinson's Hall of Fame career.

"They just wanted to get the job done," Popovich said. Few did it better than the big men around whom the Spurs built a dynasty.

06

LARRY BIRD & KEVIN McHALE

The Boston Celtics had the first overall pick in the 1980 draft, but traded down for Golden State's third overall pick, a first round pick the following year, and center Robert Parish. This move allowed Boston to draft Kevin McHale and helped form the dynasty Boston created in the 1980s.

McHale and Larry Bird were the driving forces behind a remarkable run by the Celtics in the 1980s. McHale and Bird kept the guys in charge of hanging banners in the Boston Garden pretty busy.

McHale was old school. He liked to work close to the basket, where his variety of spin moves and turnaround shots would leave defenders feeling helpless. McHale, with his long arms, was also a tremendous rebounder.

The 6-foot-9 Bird was unlike any player in the league at the time. He could drop in rainbows from way behind the three-point line, make no-look passes like a point guard, and defend the biggest guys on the floor. Teaming up with consistent center Robert Parish, McHale and Bird helped one of the greatest frontcourts in NBA history.

Bird and McHale won a championship their first year together in 1981, beating the Houston Rockets in six games. Two more titles followed.

Kevin McHale and Larry Bird teamed up in the Celtics' frontcourt for 12 seasons.

The Celtics knocked off the rival Los Angeles Lakers in 1984. Boston took care of the Rockets again in the 1986 Finals. McHale and Bird did it all in Game 6. They combined for 58 points and 21 rebounds as Boston took down Houston's centers, Ralph Sampson and Hakeem Olajuwon. They also went to the Finals two other times in the '80s but they lost to the Lakers both times.

The two friends who entered the NBA one year apart went into the Hall of Fame one year apart. Bird was inducted in 1998, with McHale going into the Hall in 1999.

05

Bob Cousy prepares to shoot over a screen set by teammate Bill Russell.

BILL RUSSELL & BOB COUSY

Bob Cousy was the NBA's first showman. The Boston Celtics point guard was called "The Houdini of the Hardwood" because he was a magician with the ball in his hands.

Cousy became one of the NBA's biggest stars from the moment he came into the league in 1950. Yet all his dribbling wizardry failed to turn the Celtics into champions during his early seasons in the NBA. Boston made the playoffs in each of Cousy's first six seasons and lost before reaching the Finals.

Bill Russell defends rival Wilt Chamberlain.

Then Bill Russell came along in 1956. Suddenly, the team that couldn't win in the playoffs became the team that couldn't lose.

The 6-foot-10 Russell and the 6-foot-1 Cousy gave the Celtics an unstoppable combination. Russell would gobble up rebounds and swat shots on defense. His career rebounding average of 22.5 per game is the second highest in league history.

While Russell served as the backbone of the defense, Cousy ran Boston's high-powered offense. Cousy paced the NBA in assists for nine straight years.

Russell and Cousy wasted little time stuffing the rafters at Boston Garden with championship banners. Boston won its first title during Russell's rookie season in 1956–57, the start of the greatest run by any team in NBA history. Russell and Cousy then led the Celtics to championships in six of the next seven seasons.

Cousy retired in 1963, but Boston kept right on rolling. The Celtics won five of the next six titles through Russell's retirement in 1969. Between 1957 and 1969, Boston won it all 11 times in 13 years.

04

Kareem Abdul-Jabbar, *left*, and Earvin Johnson were teammates for 10 years.

MAGIC JOHNSON & KAREEM ABDUL-JABBAR

Kareem Abdul-Jabbar was an NBA superstar by the time Earvin "Magic" Johnson joined him with the Los Angeles Lakers in 1979.

Johnson was pumped at the chance to play with one of the best centers in basketball history. In Johnson's NBA debut in 1979–80, Abdul-Jabbar hit a shot at the buzzer to give the Lakers the win. The 20-year-old Johnson was so excited that he gave Abdul-Jabbar a big bear-hug.

Abdul-Jabbar had a message for the rookie: calm down, we're going to win a lot of games, so don't get so worked up. The Lakers did more than win with Abdul-Jabbar in the middle and the 6-foot-9 Johnson playing point guard. They made the game so exciting that even the movie stars in nearby Hollywood took notice.

Johnson was the NBA's first big point guard. His height allowed him to see the floor over whoever was guarding him. And his ability to make behind-the-back and no-look passes brought fans to their feet.

No team made basketball look as fun and easy as the Lakers during the 1980s. They won five NBA titles with Johnson and Abdul-Jabbar working together. Johnson would run the fast break. Abdul-Jabbar would often finish possessions with his signature one-armed skyhook shot.

ALL-TIME LEADING SCORER

When Kareem Abdul-Jabbar was in college at the University of California, Los Angeles (UCLA), the National Collegiate Athletics Association (NCAA) outlawed dunking. The decision helped turn Abdul-Jabbar into an unstoppable scorer. He developed a shot called the skyhook because it seemed to drop out of the sky. He used it to score 38,387 points during his 20-year NBA career, the most by any player in basketball history.

When Los Angeles played, it wasn't just game time, it was "Showtime." The show almost always ended the same: with a win.

03

Shaquille O'Neal hugs Kobe Bryant after a game.

SHAQUILLE O'NEAL & KOBE BRYANT

Shaquille O'Neal spent the early years of his career with the Orlando Magic. The massive 7-foot-1, 310-pound center instantly became a superstar with the Magic, but in four years, he failed to win a title. Critics said maybe he didn't have what it takes to be a champion.

O'Neal moved to Los Angeles determined to prove them wrong. In the summer of 1996, he signed as a free agent with the Lakers.

The Lakers had just drafted smooth-shooting 18-year-old guard Kobe Bryant. Los Angeles hoped Bryant and O'Neal could do for the Lakers what Magic Johnson and Kareem Abdul-Jabbar did in the 1980s.

They did. It just took some time. O'Neal, Bryant, and the Lakers flamed out in the playoffs every spring until Phil Jackson arrived to become head coach in 1999. Jackson understood what it was like to get two great players to work together. He'd helped Michael Jordan and Scottie Pippen win six championships with the Chicago Bulls.

O'NEAL TO THE HEAT

The partnership between Shaquille O'Neal and Kobe Bryant ended when the Lakers traded O'Neal to the Miami Heat in 2004. Both players enjoyed success on their own late in their careers. O'Neal won a title with the Heat in 2006. Bryant guided Los Angeles to titles in 2009 and 2010.

Kobe Bryant is excited during the 2002 playoffs.

Still, the Lakers seemed to be in trouble in the 2000 Western Conference Finals. They trailed the Portland Trail Blazers by 13 points in the fourth quarter of Game 7.

Bryant and O'Neal fueled a comeback. Los Angeles stormed back to take the lead. When Bryant hit O'Neal with an alley-oop pass with 41 seconds left, the arena went crazy, and the Lakers were on their way to the Finals.

Los Angeles went on to beat the Indiana Pacers to win the first of three straight championships. O'Neal had proved his critics wrong.

02

John Stockton (12) and Karl Malone were co-MVPs of the 1993 All-Star game.

JOHN STOCKTON & KARL MALONE

John Stockton and Karl Malone met in the summer of 1984 as college students when they both tried out for the US Olympic Team. When they were cut, they ended up hanging out at lunch and helped each other get over the disappointment. They were reunited in 1985 when Malone joined Stockton with the Utah Jazz. Over the next 18 years, they formed one of the best inside/outside combinations in NBA history.

Stockton played point guard with precision and tenacity. He dished out a record 15,806 assists in his Hall of Fame career. Many of them were passes to the powerful Malone. He retired in 2004 as the second-leading scorer in NBA history.

They loved the pick-and-roll. No duo ever ran it better than Stockton and Malone. Stockton would dribble the ball and Malone would set a pick, meaning he would try to bump Stockton's defender out of the way. That forced the man guarding Malone to make a choice. He could choose to leave Malone and guard Stockton. If he did that, that would leave a smaller player on the 6-foot-9 Malone as Malone rolled to the basket. Or he could choose to stay on Malone and let Stockton drive down the lane. Either way, the Jazz had the advantage.

OLYMPIC CHAMPIONS

Though John Stockton and Karl Malone never won a championship in the NBA, their careers did come full circle. NBA players were allowed to play in the Olympics for the first time at the 1992 Games in Barcelona, Spain. Stockton and Malone were part of the "Dream Team" that won a gold medal.

Utah made the playoffs in each of the 18 seasons Stockton and Malone played together. The only thing they didn't do was win a championship. Utah reached the NBA Finals in 1997 and 1998, losing both times to the Chicago Bulls.

01

Michael Jordan drives to the rim against the Miami Heat. →

MICHAEL JORDAN & SCOTTIE PIPPEN

Michael Jordan was famous before he ever put on an NBA uniform. The guard was a 19-year-old freshman when he hit the winning jump shot that pushed North Carolina to the 1982 NCAA championship.

When Jordan joined the Chicago Bulls in 1984, his high-flying dunks earned him the nickname "Air Jordan." He made a splash early in his career, winning the Slam Dunk Contest title twice and once dropping 63 points against the Boston Celtics in the 1986 NBA playoffs.

The Bulls, though, lost that first-round series to the Celtics and star Larry Bird. In fact, they lost in the first round in each of Jordan's first three seasons.

Turns out, for all of his greatness, Jordan still needed some help. It arrived from an unlikely place.

Few people knew about lanky 6-foot-7 forward Scottie Pippen when the Bulls selected him with the fifth pick in the 1987 NBA Draft. Pippen played college basketball at the tiny University of Central Arkansas. Pippen wasn't a natural scorer like Jordan. Pippen made a name for himself with his defense and his strong all-around play.

Pippen's presence finally gave Jordan the running mate he needed. The Bulls made it out of the first round in 1988. In 1989 and 1990, they reached the Eastern Conference finals before losing to the rival Detroit Pistons.

By 1991, Jordan and Pippen were all grown up, and a modern NBA dynasty was born. Chicago brought in head coach Phil Jackson to help get Jordan, Pippen, and the rest of the Bulls over the top. Jackson understood what it took to get great players to figure out how to play together.

Though Jordan was always the bigger star, Pippen played a vital role in the team's success. One day before practice, Jackson saw Jordan and Pippen off by themselves. Pippen was helping Jordan learn a new offensive move.

"They both worked incredibly hard on their game, always putting in extra work to be better players," Jackson said. "They had an understanding of how to get a job accomplished."

Their teamwork helped Chicago go on a historic run in the 1990s. The Bulls finally reached the NBA Finals for the first time in 1991, beating Magic Johnson and the Los Angeles Lakers in five games to win the title. The win marked a changing of the guard, with the Bulls taking over as the NBA's new top team.

A year later, Chicago took care of the Portland Trail Blazers in the finals to win it all again. In 1993, Pippen and Jordan fended off good friend Charles Barkley and the Phoenix Suns for a "three-peat."

Jordan retired briefly in the fall of 1993. Pippen proved how good he was in Jordan's absence, leading the Bulls to the playoffs and finishing third in the 1994 Most Valuable Player (MVP) voting.

Michael Jordan, *right*, and Scottie Pippen won gold medals in the 1992 Olympic Games.

DEFENSIVE DUO

Though Michael Jordan is often considered the best player in basketball history, Scottie Pippen was every bit Jordan's equal when it came to defense. Jordan was named to the NBA's All-Defensive Team nine times in his career. Pippen made the All-Defensive Team eight times.

Michael Jordan and Scottie Pippen celebrate the 1997 NBA Championship.

Jordan returned to the Bulls in 1995, and by 1996, the Bulls won a record 72 games and capped off the season with another title. Chicago put together a second "three-peat," winning the title in 1996, 1997, and 1998. On their own, Jordan and Pippen were all-time greats. Together, they were an unstoppable force and the greatest duo in NBA history.

HONORABLE MENTIONS

ELVIN HAYES + WES UNSELD

Washington Bullets

The two big men combined to average 25.2 rebounds and 27.3 points per game during the 1977–78 season in leading Washington to its only NBA title.

ISIAH THOMAS + JOE DUMARS

Detroit Pistons

The "Bad Boy" Detroit Pistons of the 1980s won the NBA title in 1989 and 1990. The team, bitter rivals of Michael Jordan, beat the Chicago Bulls three years in a row in the playoffs to close out the decade.

KAREEM ABDUL-JABBAR + OSCAR ROBERTSON

Milwaukee Bucks

Before Abdul-Jabbar teamed up with Magic Johnson, the NBA's leading scorer and Robertson took the Milwaukee Bucks to its only championship in 1971 while leading the NBA with a 66-win regular season.

KEVIN DURANT + RUSSELL WESTBROOK

Oklahoma City Thunder

Durant and Westbrook put Oklahoma City on the map in the NBA, taking the Thunder to their first appearance in the NBA Finals in 2012. It was the franchise's fourth season in Oklahoma, and it finished first in a shortened NBA season with a 47–19 regular season record. But in their third straight playoff appearance, the Thunder came up short versus LeBron James and the Big Three from the Miami Heat.

MOSES MALONE + JULIUS ERVING

Philadelphia 76ers

"Dr. J" welcomed Malone as a teammate with the Philadelphia 76ers in 1982. They won only seven more games in 1982–83 than in the previous season, but they won the 1983 NBA Finals in a four-game sweep of the Los Angeles Lakers.

RALPH SAMPSON + HAKEEM OLAJUWON

Houston Rockets

The 7-foot-4 Sampson and the 7-foot Olajuwon were the original "Twin Towers" for the Houston Rockets in the 1980s. In the 1985–86 season, the Houston Rockets posted their best regular season record of the decade at 51–31, but they came up short in the finals against the Boston Celtics.

SHAWN KEMP + GARY PAYTON

Seattle SuperSonics

Gary Payton threw plenty of alley-oops to Shawn Kemp for the Seattle SuperSonics in the 1990s. They powered Seattle to a 64-win season and made it all the way to the NBA Finals in 1996.

GLOSSARY

ASSIST

A pass to a teammate that leads directly to a scored basket.

BACKCOURT

The guards on a team.

CENTER

The tallest players on a basketball court. Centers typically play close to the basket.

DRAFT

A system that allows teams to acquire new players coming into a league.

DUNK

To jam the ball through the hoop with one or two hands.

FORWARD

Bigger players who are versatile and can both rebound and shoot.

FRONTCOURT

The forwards on a team.

GUARD

Usually a smaller player who can shoot from long range and pass the ball to teammates.

REBOUND

Grabbing a ball after a missed shot.

ROOKIE

A first-year player in the NBA.

THREE-POINTER

Any shot taken behind the three-point line.

MORE INFORMATION

ONLINE RESOURCES

Booklinks
NONFICTION NETWORK
FREE! ONLINE NONFICTION RESOURCES

To learn more about the NBA's greatest duos, visit **abdobooklinks.com**. These links are routinely monitored and updated to provide the most current information available.

BOOKS

Bryant, Howard. *Legends: The Best Players, Games, and Teams in Basketball*. New York: Philomel Books, 2017.

Kramer, S. A. *Basketball's Greatest Players*. New York: Random House, 2015.

Rivkin, Jennifer. *All Ball: Basketball's Greatest Players*. New York: Crabtree Publishing Company, 2016.

PLACE TO VISIT

NAISMITH MEMORIAL BASKETBALL HALL OF FAME

1000 Hall of Fame Avenue
Springfield, MA 01105
877-446-6752
hoophall.com

The Basketball Hall of Fame is like a museum dedicated to basketball. It highlights the greatest players, coaches, and moments in the sport's history. Many of the players mentioned in this book are enshrined there. It is home to more than 300 inductees and more than 40,000 square feet of basketball history.

INDEX

ABOUT THE AUTHOR

Will Graves grew up in the Washington, DC, suburbs rooting every year for the Washington Bullets (now the Wizards) to win an NBA title. He's still waiting. In the meantime, Graves has spent over two decades as a sportswriter. He works for the Associated Press in Pittsburgh, Pennsylvania, where he covers the NFL, the NHL, and Major League Baseball when he's not teaching his son the art of the three-pointer.